A Great Idea

Sunscreen for Plants

by Carla Mooney

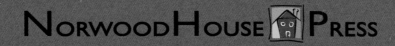

NorwoodHousePress

Norwood House Press
PO Box 316598
Chicago, Illinois 60631

For information regarding Norwood House Press, please visit our Web site at:

www.norwoodhousepress.com or call 866-565-2900.

LIBRARY OF CONGRESS CATALOGING-IN-PUBLICATION DATA

Mooney, Carla, 1970–
 Sunscreen for plants : a great idea / Carla Mooney.
   p. cm.
 Includes bibliographical references and index.
 Summary: "Purshade is a new SPF 45 spray that can be applied to crops in
order to prevent burning and dehydration"--Provided by publisher.
 ISBN-13: 978-1-59953-344-5 (library ed. : alk. paper)
 ISBN-10: 1-59953-344-8 (library ed. : alk. paper) 1. Plants—Effect of solar radiation
on--Juvenile literature. 2. Plants, Protection of—Juvenile literature. 3. Sunscreens
(Cosmetics)—Juvenile literature. 4. Sunburn—Juvenile literature. I. Title.
 S600.7.S65M66 2009
 632'.12—dc22
                                                              2009015641

Manufactured in the United States of America.

Contents

Note: Words that are **bolded** in the text are defined in the glossary on page 43.

Chapter 1

A Growing Problem

Most people know that a day at the beach with no sunscreen is dangerous. But did you know that a hot, sunny day can be just as dangerous for plants? Plants can burn in the sun just like people. Apple and pear skins can get brown. Grapes can **shrivel** on the vine. Even thick-skinned pineapples can get a sunburn!

So in June 2008, when the temperature began to rise in Southern California, growers got nervous. Normally, the area around San Diego is a comfortable 75°F to 80°F (24°C to 27°C). This time, the heat soared much higher. In some places, the temperature rose to over 100°F (38°C). **Avocado** growers watched their trees. It was hot at the wrong time for avocados. The heat wave lasted for almost a week. By the time things cooled down, the damage was done. The sun and heat had destroyed the fruit as it was beginning to mature on the trees. Some avocado farmers lost more than half of their crop. Even worse, the heat harmed the flower buds on the avocado trees. These flowers were going to produce the next year's fruit. Now there would be fewer avocados the next year, too.

These California avocados can be harmed when the weather is unseasonably hot.

Avocados are not the only plants hurt by too much sun and heat. The sun can harm all types of fruits and vegetables. In December 2007, a heat wave hurt crops in Australia. The sun burned lettuce leaves. It shriveled grapes on the vine. Apple and pear growers had to throw away one out of every five pieces of fruit. Some people said that burned plums looked like they had been sprayed with a blowtorch. One grape grower said that he lost almost half of his grapes. Losing that many grapes was going to cost him a lot of money. He was afraid he would have to sell his vineyard. Even supermarket shoppers felt the heat. If they wanted to buy fruit, they

Photosynthesis

Photosynthesis

light

oxygen

carbon dioxide

water

Photosynthesis is how plants make food (sugars) using the energy from the sun. The plant uses sugar as fuel for growing. In photosynthesis, plants take in carbon dioxide from the air. They use sunlight to turn the carbon dioxide and water into sugar and oxygen. The sugar moves through tubes in the plant. It travels to the plant's roots, stem, and fruit. The plant uses some of the sugar for energy right away. The rest of it is stored in the plant. Plants let out the oxygen into the air. Animals and humans use this oxygen to breathe.

would have to settle for smaller pieces or fruit with spots.

Too Much of a Good Thing

Plants need the sun to photosynthesize and produce flowers and fruit. Not every plant needs the same amount of sun. Unexpected weather that is too hot or too dry at the wrong time can have a devastating effect on plants. Sometimes, sunlight can be too much of a good thing.

Too much sun hurts plants. The sun's **ultraviolet** rays can burn them just as they burn people's skin. The skin of sunburned fruit can blister and get spots. Most people do not like to buy fruit with spots. Shoppers will pass over spotted fruit to buy pieces that look perfect. Supermarkets know the spotted fruit is not going to sell

as easily. They will not pay growers as much for spotted fruit. Severe sunburn can also change the way fruit tastes. A burned piece of fruit may have a different color inside its skin. It may also have a different firmness and be less juicy.

Plants can also be stressed by the heat. When plants get too hot, they sweat just like people. This process is called **transpiration**. Sweating helps to cool the plant. But if the plant loses too much water, it will become **dehydrated**. When a person gets overheated and dehydrated, his or her body might shut down with heat exhaustion. That is the body's way of trying to save itself and its brain. Plants react the same way to heat stress. With less water, the plant's photosynthesis process slows down or even stops. This helps the plant survive. Instead of using its energy to make fruit, it uses its water and energy to stay alive. Plants under heat stress produce smaller pieces of fruit. They also do not grow as many pieces.

Farm workers grade apples to select which ones will go to market and which will become juice.

Losing Money Because of the Sun

Sun-damaged crops sell for less money. When fruit is picked, growers sort the pieces by how each one looks. Fruit that looks perfect and has good color goes in the first pile and sells as ready-to-eat pieces. They become the fruit and vegetables in the supermarket's **produce** section. These pieces need to look good so that shoppers will want to buy them. For growers, selling to the ready-to-eat market earns the most money.

Growers sort the fruit with damage and sunburn into a second pile. This pile gets sold to make items like juice and applesauce. A shopper never sees the fruit that makes juice or sauce. That is why these fruits do not need to look as good. This market, however, pays growers less money for their fruit. Each damaged plant causes farmers to lose money.

Getting Worse

Farmers have dealt with plant sunburn for years. But recently, the problem seems to be getting worse. Scientists think that **climate** change and a growing population are both to blame. The planet is slowly getting warmer. Also, the part of the atmosphere

Is It Getting Hotter in Here?

Many scientists are worried that the earth is getting hotter. They think that this is happening because there is more carbon dioxide in the air than ever before. In the past century, people around the world have been burning more fossil fuels. Fossil fuels include coal, oil, and natural gas. When fossil fuels burn, they release carbon dioxide into the air. Carbon dioxide traps heat in the atmosphere. When that happens, temperatures rise.

At the same time, people are cutting down many forests. This is bad because trees help reduce carbon dioxide in two ways. First, they use it for photosynthesis. They also provide shade so people do not have to use as much energy to cool homes and offices. From 1990 to 2005, the world lost 3 percent of its forests. Without these trees, more carbon dioxide stays in the air, and the earth warms even faster.

that protects the earth from the sun, the ozone layer, has gotten thinner. This allows more of the sun's rays to reach the earth's surface. Plants and people are more likely to get burned.

Most plants and trees can only grow in certain areas. How hot and cold it gets in an area helps determine whether a plant can grow there. As areas get warmer, certain fruits and vegetables may no longer grow well. For example, California is known for growing lots of grapes to make **premium** wines. But that may change if California gets even a few degrees hotter. Some scientists predict that parts of California will no longer be able to grow the premium-wine grapes.

The population is growing at a fast pace as well. As people take up more space, there is less land for farming. Farmers have to figure out ways to grow more crops in less space. They also will not be able to move to another location easily if the climate gets too hot to grow their plants.

Lou Bennett grows grapes in Victoria, a state in southeast Australia. He saw firsthand the effect of stronger sun and heat on his plants. In early 2009, a record-

A worker prunes grapevines that have been scorched by the heat.

making heat wave struck his town. Bennett watched the thermometer hit 100°F (38°C) for 12 straight days. He knew his grape vines were in trouble. The sun was scorching the life out of his plants. One morning, two whole fields of plants were wiped out. In total, Bennett says that the sun burned about one of every three of his grapes. A bad grape crop means less money for Bennett. As a result, he has had to let his farmhands go. Now Bennett works the field, and his children help after school.

Protecting Plants

Plant sunburn and heat stress are not going away. In fact, many scientists believe it is only going to get worse. Some growers set up shade nets over their plants to shield

Walnuts show the effects of too much sun. With climate change leading to drought, some farmers are turning to sunscreen to protect their crops.

them from the sun. Nets could cover a **greenhouse** roof and shade all the plants inside. But they were not a good solution for growers with larger fields. The nets were hard to install and were expensive for large farms and **orchards**, which had to install a large number of them.

Some farmers sprayed or misted their crops with water. This method is called

Harmful Radiation

In recent years, more of the sun's harmful rays are hitting the planet. This is happening because the earth's ozone layer has gotten thinner. The ozone layer is a part of the atmosphere that acts like a giant sunshade. It absorbs most of the sun's harmful ultraviolet, or UV, rays. As the layer gets thinner it is not able to absorb harmful radiation as well. As a result, more UV rays reach the earth.

Why did the ozone layer get thinner? Scientists believe that human-made chemicals slowly eroded it. Some of these chemicals are called chlorofluorocarbons (CFCs). CFCs were used to keep things cold in refrigerators and air conditioners. They were also used to make soaps and foam. When CFC gases entered the air, they caused the ozone layer to shrink.

Many countries wanted to stop the damage to the ozone layer. They decided to ban or limit CFCs. The United States was one of those countries. But even though many people have stopped using CFCs, the problem is still there. That is because CFCs last a long time. CFC gases from years ago may keep harming the ozone layer for many years to come. Today scientists are working with companies to make more ozone-friendly chemicals. They hope the ozone layer will begin to recover soon.

These refrigerators may have contained harmful CFCs that scientists believe have contributed to the thinning of the ozone layer.

evaporative cooling. It helped to keep the plants cooler in hot weather. Cooler plants meant less heat stress damage. Still it was not the best solution. Misting the fields and trees used a lot of water. In many areas, water is scarce. When temperatures get really high, many towns ask people not to use as much water. Spraying all this water on large areas of crops just seemed wasteful. In California scarce water supplies led officials to put farmers under tight water restrictions. Without enough water to spray on their fields, farmers know their crops will not grow as well.

A New Idea

Growers kept thinking about new ways to protect plants from the sun. They kept coming back to the same idea. Plants and people react in similar ways to the sun. When people spend too much time in the sun, they burn. So do plants. When people get hot, they sweat. Plants also sweat to cool off. Both people and plants need more water when they are hot and sweaty. If they do not get it, both get sick. People use sunscreen to protect themselves from the sun. How great would it be if there was a sunscreen for plants?

Did You Know?

Plants breathe through tiny holes called **stomata**. The stomata are on the underside of the plant's leaves.

Early Plant Sunscreens

At first, people tried plant sunscreens made from clay. Clay is one of the oldest sunscreens. One type of clay is called kaolin. This soft, white mineral clay is found in nature. It is also generally safe to use on food. Clay-based sunscreens were powders. They could be mixed with water and sprayed on fruit, leaves, and bark. When the water dried, a white film was left behind on the plant's leaves or fruit. The white film provided some protection from the sun's rays.

Sometimes though, the clay protected the plant too much. Plants need sunlight to grow. Clay sunscreens blocked all the sun's rays, good and bad. Clay sunscreens also had several other drawbacks. First, they washed off in the rain. This meant that growers needed to reapply the clay sunscreen. It also meant that clay sunscreens could not be used with evaporative cooling. Also, minerals in the rain or water sometimes caused the clay sunscreen to stick to the fruit in spots. These splotches of white film were hard to remove. This gave the fruit a blotchy color. Blotchy fruit did not look good to buyers. Finally, clay sunscreens were not always easy to apply. Sometimes the sunscreen foamed and formed globs in the spray tanks.

Other people tried a mix of clay and wax sunscreens on apples. Wax sunscreens provided some protection from sunburn. These sunscreens did not cause blotches on the fruit like clay-only sunscreens did. Instead, they formed a waxy **residue** that you could eat. The wax sunscreens did not wash off easily in the rain.

This farmer sprays his apple trees with water to prevent them from being scorched by the sun.

This meant growers could still use evaporative cooling on their plants.

But wax had its drawbacks too. First, it could not be mixed with other products, such as fertilizers. If a wax sunscreen was mixed with a calcium-based fertilizer or other product, for example, it turned thick and lumpy like cottage cheese. Growers had to make separate trips to the field to spray first the fertilizer and then the sunscreen.

Sunscreens aren't the only sprays growers use. Other sprays fertilize the

One of the first signs of a sun-damaged plant is a duller leaf color. The green plant will also have an overall grayish color.

plants or protect them against bugs and disease. The wax sunscreens made it hard to use the other sprays. The wax formed a barrier between the plant and other sprays.

Also, some chemical sprays stuck to the wax sunscreens. This made it harder to wash off the chemicals before the fruit went to customers.

Wax sunscreens also did not do a good job of reducing heat stress on plants. In fact, wax absorbed the heat from the sun's radiation. This made the plant hotter. Growers still needed to use water and evaporative cooling to fight the heat.

Not everyone was happy with these early sunscreens. So some researchers decided to keep trying new ways to make a sunscreen for plants.

Chapter 2

A New Type of Sunscreen

David Cope spent a lot of time with fruit and vegetable growers. Cope is the president of a company called Purfresh. For years, his company helped growers after they **harvested** their crop. His company developed ways to help growers wash and remove harmful bacteria from their produce. The company also created ways to keep the fruit fresher

David Cope had a new idea on how to protect plants from too much sun.

David Cope listens to farmers talk about the damage done to their crops from too much sun. This kind of information helped Cope come up with the idea of sunscreen for plants.

while it was being packed, stored, and shipped to buyers.

But growers kept talking about problems they were having before harvest. Too much sun and heat damaged the fruit. Too many pieces had to be thrown away unused. Harvests were also getting smaller because of the sun. Cope walked around fields and orchards. He saw firsthand the problems growers were having. He had heard about how a changing climate was making things hotter. That meant the growers' sun problems would only get worse. They needed a solution, and fast.

Cope talked to the engineers at his company. They decided that the best way to help growers would be to make a new sunscreen for plants. A plant sunscreen would help the plants stay cooler during the hot months. It would protect them from sunburn. But the sunscreen needed to be easy to use. Growers did not want to make a separate trip to the field to spray the sunscreen. They wanted a spray they could mix with something they were already spraying on their plants. The sunscreen also needed to wash off easily. No one wanted to see it when the fruit was ready to ship to buyers.

Did You Know?

The first commercially available human sunscreen was introduced in the United States in 1928.

In 2006 Cope and his team set out to learn about sunscreens. They studied the different materials in them. They wanted to figure out what would work best for plants.

Trying Something New

Cope and a team of engineers then studied the other types of plant sunscreens such as clay and wax. They looked to see what was working and what was not. Then they decided it was time to try something new. They wanted to design a plant sunscreen that was clean and green. That means they did not want to use human-made chemicals. Instead, they wanted to use nature's own power to protect plants. They believed that nature had been **self-sufficient** for a long time. So why not look to nature for a solution?

A material called calcium carbonate proved to be part of the answer. Rocks and minerals all over the world hold calcium carbonate. Limestone rocks are ac-

Calcium carbonate proved to be an ideal mineral to add to plant sunscreen.

Other Uses for Calcium Carbonate

Plant sunscreens are not the only products that use calcium carbonate. It is found in many everyday items:

- cement
- blackboard chalk
- diapers
- glossy paper coatings
- household scouring powders
- ceramics glaze
- antacids
- calcium supplements
- toothpaste

tually made of it. Crushing limestone creates a powdery form of the mineral. This powder is used in many products—from paper to toothpaste. Cope's team thought that using calcium carbonate in a sunscreen was a good choice. Nature made it. It was easy to find and did not cost a lot of money. Most importantly, it could reflect the harmful light but still let in the helpful light from the sun.

Using Crystals to Reflect Light

Calcium carbonate crystals are called **calcite**. The team realized that these crystals act like tiny mirrors. These mirrors can reflect the sun's harmful UV rays. Calcite crystals come in hundreds of shapes, sizes, and colors. Each type of crystal reflects light in a different way. So the team began testing different crystals. They wanted to find out which type would work the best to shield plants from the sun.

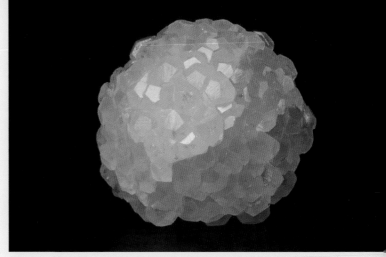

The crystal formations in this chunk of calcium carbonate are clearly visible. The rock has the ability to reflect light and so became a good choice to add to plant sunscreen.

Before long, Cope's team tested a calcium sunscreen. It was called Eclipse and worked well for apple growers in the Pacific Northwest. While working with Eclipse, the team learned a lot about calcium carbonate and how it worked. They used that knowledge to create a new sunscreen for more types of plants. They named

Hippopotamus Sunscreen

Almost all plants and animals need protection from the sun's hot rays. But how many make their own sunscreen? That is what a hippopotamus does. The first time you see a hippo covered in a red, oily substance, you might think it is bleeding. It is not. The red substance is actually a type of sweat. The hippo's red sweat is a do-it-yourself sunscreen. It has microscopic structures that scatter light. This protects the hippos from burning in the sun. The red color comes from red and orange pigments in the sweat. These pigments also protect the hippo by absorbing ultraviolet light.

This hippo's sweat causes him to turn red.

their sunscreen Purshade. It could be used on more types of plants and in more places than Eclipse could. The new liquid sunscreen worked by forming a film on the plants. The thin film was made of millions of tiny crystals. Each crystal acted like a **prism** or a mirror. They reflected most of the sun's harmful rays away from the plant. But they still allowed in the good sun rays for photosynthesis.

Testing Around the World

Cope's team tested the sunscreen all around the world. Grape growers in Europe tried it on their vines. Growers in Chile sprayed it on apples and wine grapes. In the United States, growers in Florida and California tested the new sunscreen on peppers, grapes, walnuts, tomatoes, and melons. In each place, growers reported that they had a lot less sun damage on the plants sprayed with the new sunscreen. The protected plants grew bigger and better fruit. They also grew more pieces, or higher yields, of fruit.

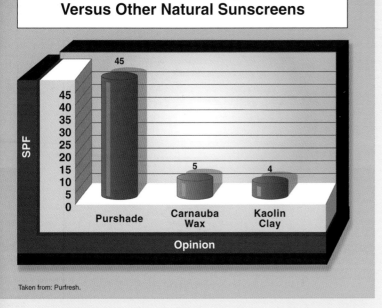

SPF (Sun Protection Factor) of Purshade Versus Other Natural Sunscreens

SPF

45

45
40
35
30
25
20
15
10
5
0

5

4

Purshade | Carnauba Wax | Kaolin Clay

Opinion

Taken from: Purfresh.

Purshade was pretty exciting for growers. It had a protection rating of SPF 45. That was 10 times higher than other plant sunscreens. It was a liquid and could be easily mixed and applied. Pur-shade could also be mixed with other sprays that growers already used. That meant growers did not have to spend extra time in the field to spray the sunscreen. They also did not have to buy new equipment. They could use the nozzles and tanks they already had. After the harvest, the new sunscreen washed off the fruit easily.

In 2008 word spread about the new sunscreen for plants. In an interview, Dave Cope talked about the idea behind his company's sunscreens. He said, "We wanted to figure out ways to harness the power of nature to do something good. That's what our sunscreens do."

Chapter 3

Protecting Crops Around the World

Patrick Gibbons and his brother Mike grow apples in the Yakima Valley. The Yakima Valley sits in central Washington State. It is known as the apple capital of the world. The Gibbonses' apple trees cover 100 acres (0.4 sq. km) of land. An acre (4,047 sq. m) of land is about the same size as a football

Gala apples ripen in the sun. If too much sun causes the apples to develop brown spots, the farmer will be unable to sell them to markets.

field. So 100 acres might seem like a big orchard, but actually, the Gibbonses' orchard is one of the small ones. Some of the biggest apple orchards grow fruit on 4,000 acres!

Protecting Apples

Growing apples is a challenge. Apples are graded by their size and color. Bigger apples with the best color sell for higher prices. To get better color, the apples need sunshine. So the Gibbonses pruned their apple trees to let in more light. But this also had a downside: More sunlight also meant more sunburn on the apples.

Then the Gibbonses heard about the calcium carbonate sunscreen called Purshade. They liked the idea of using a calcium-based sunscreen. When a grower sprays a liquid, about 75 percent actually hits the trees and fruit. The rest scatters in the wind and covers the ground. A sunscreen spray needed to be safe for the trees and soil. The Gibbonses knew the new sunscreen would not hurt anything

How Does a Plant Move Water?

In people, veins and arteries carry blood to every part of the body. They are part of our **circulatory system**. Our blood moves from the tips of our fingers to the bottom of our toes. Plants do not have blood, but they need to move water. That is when a plant's xylem gets ready to work. Inside a plant, tubes called xylem carry water. Xylem are like a plant's circulatory system. If a tree's leaves need water, the xylem zip it from the roots all the way up to the top of the tree. The xylem have another job, too. They also help support the plant so it can stand tall. Xylem tissue dies and regrows every year and forms the rings you see in a tree trunk.

Red dye has circulated through this celery stem's xylem.

else in their orchard. The calcium in it would actually help the trees and soil.

The Gibbonses sprayed the sunscreen on their apples. As the apples grew, the Gibbonses saw how the sunscreen protected the fruit. The apples were bigger and had good color. The sunscreen also washed off easily and did not leave a white film. People would like these apples better. They looked delicious to eat.

Today the Gibbons brothers think plant sunscreens are a great idea. They plan to use plant sunscreen every year at their orchard.

Improving Crops

Tests proved the Purshade sunscreen cooled a plant's leaves 7 to 10 degrees. That might not seem like a big difference. Still even that small amount of cooling helped the plant be healthier. A healthier plant can grow better fruit.

As word spread, more growers around the world sprayed the plant sunscreens on their crops. Different crops grew bigger and better. Corn growers in Thailand harvested more **bushels** per acre. Honeydew

Did You Know?

Sunburned leaves stay on the plant. They usually look off-color or slightly yellowed. Sometimes, the leaf will get small bumps on the yellowish area.

A walnut grower examines his crop. Many growers are using sunscreen to protect their vulnerable crops from heat.

growers in Mexico grew bigger melons. Tomato growers in Australia had a lot fewer sun-damaged plants.

Grape growers were also excited about plant sunscreens. Dick Cooper is a wine grape grower near Sacramento, California. He runs Cooper Vineyards with his son-in-law Dave Cheetham. Cooper says that grapes have a natural way to protect themselves from the sun. They grow a

canopy of leaves that shades the fruit. Sometimes, however, the canopy is not big or thick enough. Then sunlight gets in and burns the fruit. Too much sun also makes the grapevines too hot. Hot vines do not use their water to make leaves and fruit. Cooper says that grapes end up

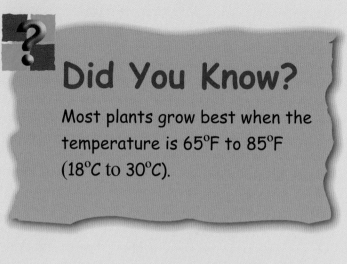
A vineyard owner looks over his grapes. Like many farmers, he has chosen to protect the delicate grapes with sunscreen.

looking like an olive pit when they get too much sun.

Cooper and Cheetham decided to give the Purshade plant sunscreen a try. They saw an immediate improvement in their grapes. The sunscreen protected the grapes and did not cause any problems when it was time to make wine. Both men were impressed with the good results. They also liked how simple it was to use the sunscreen. Cooper and Cheetham consider the test of plant sunscreens a success. Today it is an important part of their grape-growing business.

Healthier Plants

Dave Cheetham knew the sunscreen helped protect his grapes from the sun. He also believed the sunscreens helped to make his plants healthier. To prove it, he attached a special tracking device to his plants. The device measured how often the plants respired, or breathed in, carbon dioxide for photosynthesis. Cheetham found that plants with sunscreen were indeed healthier. They were able to keep respiring even during the hottest part of the day. Plants that were not treated with sunscreen stopped respiring. They shut down because they were too hot.

Sunscreens and Bugs

Some plant sunscreens can protect plants from more than the sun. They can help plants ward off unwanted bugs. The tiny particles in sunscreens reflect light and repel the bugs. When bugs land on the plant, tiny sunscreen particles stick to their bodies. This makes them upset and they fly away. Some bugs that cannot fly become confused when the particles stick to them. Confused bugs might not lay eggs or feed on the plant. Also, when the tiny particles reflect the sun, it gives the plant a disguise. The bugs sometimes do not recognize the fruit or plant. The bugs will fly away and look for another target.

Better Prices for Everyone

Plant sunscreens can help growers make more money. Tests with tomato growers

This worker is spraying grapevines with sunscreen to protect the harvest from sunburn.

This savings can get passed on to supermarkets. Then the markets can lower the prices for shoppers, and everyone wins.

Winning Awards

People saw how much plant sunscreens helped growers. In 2008 *Time* magazine named Purshade one of its 50 Best Inventions of the Year. Every year, the magazine looks for inventions that are a new idea. They also look for inventions that meet needs that have not been met before. The magazine believed that plant sunscreen was a simple and smart idea. It was an invention that made people's lives better.

show plants with sunscreen grew almost $2,000 more fruit per acre (4,047 sq. m). If they have more fruit to sell, growers can charge less money for each piece.

Chapter 4

Plant Sunscreens in the Future

Today the only people who use plant sunscreens are farmers who have large orchards or fields of crops. Someday soon that might change. Neighborhood stores might carry plant sunscreens right next to other garden supplies. Home gardeners then would be able to buy a sunscreen for their backyard gardens. Homegrown plants would all be protected from the sun just like large commercial crops.

Growing Organically

Scientists are also working on ways to make plant sunscreen that can be used by **organic** food growers. An organic food has to be made or grown a certain way. Organic growers cannot use most chemicals on their food. It also cannot be genetically modified. That means scientists cannot have changed the plant's genes to make it grow bigger or better.

For many years, small family farms grew organic foods. These farms usually sold their crops at farmers markets. In recent years, organic food has grown more popular. Now you can buy organic fruits and vegetables at the supermarket.

Organic growers cannot use current plant sunscreens. This is because the sun-

Many farmers markets, like this one in San Francisco, feature organic food.

Organic Farming

Modern farmers have practiced organic farming since the late 1940s. The first organic gardens were small. Today, organic gardens have grown into large farms. Most people know that organic farms do not use certain chemicals or pesticides. But organic farming is more than that. It is a system of farming. Organic farmers believe healthy, fertile soil grows the best plants. Healthy, strong plants can better fight disease and pests. To keep their soils fertile, the farmers rotate crops. They also plant cover crops like rye, alfalfa, or clover after harvest to protect the soil from weeds, insects, and disease. Organic farmers also spread **compost** over the soil to naturally fertilize it. Cotton, flowers, grains, fruits, and vegetables are some of the products that can be grown organically.

Organic farmers like this one must apply strict standards to their growing methods.

screens have preservatives in them. A preservative is a chemical added to something to keep it fresh. The preservatives in plant sunscreens are not organic. But some preservatives, such as salt, sugar, and vinegar, are natural. Natural preservatives can be used with organic foods. Scientists are working with these natural preservatives. They are trying to make an organic version of plant sunscreens. That way more types of growers will be able to protect their plants from the sun.

Designing Customized Sunscreens

The sun affects each type of plant in a different way. An apple tree and a lettuce plant will each have a different reaction to the same sun. Where a plant grows also affects how it reacts to the sun. What is the **altitude** of the farm? How hot does it get? How intense is the ultraviolet radiation? How much does it rain? All of these details affect how plants grow and react to the sun.

Today there are only a few types of plant sunscreens. Scientists hope to make more. Someday there might be a sunscreen for each type of plant. Scientists know that the tiny particle mirrors in plant sunscreens reflect light. What if they changed the size and shape of those particles? They could change how the sunscreen reflects light. These changes could be made for specific plants and places. The **customized** sunscreens would better protect each plant according to where it lives.

Water Conservation

Plant sunscreens might also help growers better use water in the future. In many areas of the world, drought is a big problem. A drought happens when less rain than usual falls over a long period of time. Usually a drought happens over several months or longer. Droughts do not just hit hot, dry places. They can strike anywhere in the world.

During a drought, farmers do not have enough water in the soil for their plants to grow normally. Nearby streams, rivers, and lakes may shrink or dry up altogether.

Drought in places like Australia (pictured) has made water for farms scarce.

The Dust Bowl

One of the most famous droughts in United States' history is known as the Dust Bowl. It took place over several years in the 1930s. The drought hit areas of Kansas, Colorado, Oklahoma, New Mexico, and Texas. Without water, the soil dried out. Crops died in the fields. Droughts had happened before in these areas. This time it was worse than ever before. In earlier years, farmers removed natural grasses to farm and graze cattle on the plains. These grasses had acted as anchors for the soil. Now that the grasses were gone, the dry soil had nothing to keep it in place. It turned to dust and blew away in large, dark clouds. People called these enormous dust storms "black blizzards." Sometimes the dust clouds were so big, they reached cities on the East Coast such as New York and Washington, D.C. It grew so bad in the Dust Bowl that many farmers abandoned their farms. They moved their families to other states to get a fresh start.

A huge dust storm in Stratford, Texas, shows the effects of the Dust Bowl in the 1930s.

Did You Know?

A particle film sunscreen, like Purshade, is **porous**. Water and carbon dioxide can pass through the film. The plant can respire, or breathe, normally.

screen reflects the sun's rays and keeps the plant cooler. A cooler plant needs less water. It can also better use water to grow and produce fruit. This can help growers produce healthier crops during a drought.

In some droughts, the government will restrict the use of water. They might not let the farmers use extra water on their plants.

Plants need water to grow. The hotter a plant gets the more water it needs. Also when a plant uses its water to keep cool, it is not using the water to grow or produce fruit.

Scientists hope that plant sunscreens will be one way to **conserve** water. A plant sun-

World Food Shortages

In some countries, sun damage to crops can be devastating. In Africa, for example, severe drought and sun has ruined many crops. Many African countries face food shortages, and often they cannot afford to buy food from their neighbors. When this happens, the people of these countries do not have enough to eat. Some starve. Scientists hope that one day plant sunscreens will help these countries. Being able to grow more food could help keep people around the world from going hungry.

A farmer sprays water on a crop of lettuce. Plants can absorb minerals in the soil once water dissolves them.

Improving Plant Nutrition

Plant sunscreens may also become a new way to deliver **nutrients** to plants. Your body needs vitamins and minerals to be healthy and strong. Plants also need minerals. The plant uses mineral nutrients to grow, fight disease, and make leaves and fruit. They find them in the soil. Water in the soil dissolves the minerals. Then the plant's roots absorb them. Often, there are not enough mineral nutrients in the soil. That is when farmers have to use fertilizers, which add nutrients to the soil.

Calcium is an important nutrient for plant growth. One way plants use calcium is to build plant cell walls. Just like calcium builds strong bones in people, it helps plants build a strong structure.

Many growers add calcium to their soil so their crops can be strong and healthy.

Plant sunscreens are a new way to supply calcium to plants. The new sunscreens have calcium carbonate in them. When growers spray their plants, some of the sunscreen spray hits the soil. The added calcium in the soil can then be absorbed by the plants. Scientists studying plant sunscreen have found that getting more calcium is a good thing for plants. It helps plants grow firmer, better fruit. Maybe in the future, plant sunscreens will be an easy way to give more nutrients to plants.

One Plant at a Time

Plant sunscreens may not be able to save every plant from sun damage. But they can improve plant health in many places. The list of benefits is long. Healthier plants grow more food. They produce bigger and better fruit. They make better use of their water. With the planet's climate changing, water and resources are getting harder to find. Plant sunscreens can help growers change with the planet. They can grow crops in hotter, drier weather. This may help avoid food shortages and higher prices in the future.

David Cope thinks it is only a matter of time before more people realize that plant sunscreens are a great idea. There are lots of people who wonder what they did before there was sunscreen for people. Maybe someday, they will feel the same way about sunscreen for plants.

Glossary

altitude: How high a location is above sea level.

avocado: A pear-shaped fruit with green to black skin, creamy greenish-yellow flesh, and a large pit.

bushels: Units of dry measure each equal to 35.24 liters, or 32 dry quarts.

calcite: One of the most common minerals, known as calcium carbonate or $CaCO_3$. It is often found in a crystal form.

canopy: A covering suspended over an object.

circulatory system: The system that circulates blood and lymph through the body, consisting of the heart, blood vessels, blood, lymph, and the lymphatic vessels and glands.

climate: Weather conditions like temperature, rainfall, and wind that are common in a given area.

compost: A mixture of dead leaves or manure that is used to fertilize soil.

conserve: To use something carefully to avoid wasting it.

customized: Made with unique features for a specific purpose.

dehydrated: Having lost water or body fluids.

evaporative cooling: A technique used by growers to cool plants and trees by spraying or misting with water.

greenhouse: A structure, usually made of glass or plastic, where plants are grown and protected.

harvested: Picked or gathered in a ripe crop.

nutrients: A source of nourishment, or the nourishing ingredients in food.

orchards: A group of trees that grows fruit or nuts.

organic: Grown without the use of human-made chemicals, drugs, or hormones.

porous: Full of tiny holes called pores.

premium: Having better quality or value than others of the same kind.

prism: A transparent object, usually of glass or plastic, that can separate white light passed through it into the spectrum of colors (like a rainbow) and reflect them.

produce: Agricultural products, especially fruits and vegetables.

residue: Something left behind after a chemical or physical process like evaporation or combustion has taken place.

self-sufficient: Being able to provide for your own needs without help from anyone else.

shrivel: Become or make shrunken and wrinkled, often by drying.

stomata: Small holes on plant leaves through which gases enter and exit the plant.

transpiration: The evaporation of water from a plant's leaves, flowers, stem, and roots.

ultraviolet: Sunlight that has wavelengths shorter than the human eye can see.

For More Information

Web Sites

Biology4Kids: Plant Basics (www.biology4kids.com/files/plants_main.html). This Web site uses kid-friendly language to explain concepts like photosynthesis, plant structure, and plant systems.

Drought for Kids (http://drought.unl.edu/kids/index.htm). This Web site gives lots of information about drought, tracking drought, how it affects us, and ideas to reduce our risk from drought.

Newton's Apple: Photosynthesis (www.newtonsapple.tv/TeacherGuide.php?id=915#activity). This Web site answers science questions. The photosynthesis page includes a teacher's guide, kids' activity, and a video clip about plants and photosynthesis.

Purfresh (www.purfresh.com). This Web site gives detailed explanations of how Purshade and Eclipse plant sunscreens work and their results in the field.

SunWise Kids (www.epa.gov/sunwise/kids.html). This Web site gives lots of kid-friendly information about the sun, UV radiation, and the ozone layer. It gives action steps for sun protection. The site also has an interactive game about sun protection.

Index

About the Author

Carla Mooney lives in Pittsburgh, Pennsylvania with her husband and three children. She received a bachelor of economics degree from the University of Pennsylvania. She currently works as a freelance writer and has written several books and articles for young readers.